NOT OK?

Prologue

There comes a moment when the world feels like it's splitting apart. The things that once made sense seem incomprehensible, and the things you once trusted crumble under the weight of dissonance. It presses heavily, an invisible force that seems to fill the air, your mind, even your breath. Chaos surrounds you, echoes within you, and the harder you try to grasp for order, the more it seems to slip away. In these moments, it's easy to believe that dissonance is the enemy—that it must be silenced, escaped, or destroyed. But dissonance is not the enemy. It is the signal.

When things are not OK, the world is not betraying you. It is calling to you. It is asking you to look closer, to sit with what is fractured and unclear, and to begin seeing the patterns within the chaos. This is not an easy process, nor a quick one. Chaos does not resolve on demand, nor does clarity arrive simply because we want it to. But this process is essential. Dissonance is not a failure; it is the place where transformation begins.

To live is to encounter dissonance, again and again. It is woven into the human condition, as natural as breath, as constant as change. But when we encounter dissonance, our instinct is often to run. We try to avoid it, to bury it, to pretend it doesn't exist. Or we try to fight it, to impose order on it, to force resolution before its lessons have been learned. In both cases, we miss the opportunity dissonance brings. Because within every fracture, every tension, every unresolved moment, there is something waiting to be discovered—a signal that points us toward growth, understanding, and alignment.

This book is not here to tell you how to make things OK. It is not a guide to fixing your life, nor a prescription for resolving dissonance. It is here to meet you where you are—in the chaos, in the fractures, in the places where things do not align. It is here to help you listen. What is the tension teaching you? What can the fractures reveal? And how, even in the deepest chaos, might you begin to find clarity?

To face dissonance is not to conquer it, but to understand it. It is to recognize that the parts of your life that feel most broken are also the parts that hold the greatest potential for transformation. Chaos is not the end of the story; it is where the story begins. Every fracture is an opening. Every tension is a bridge. And even when things are not OK, there is a path forward—not away from the dissonance, but through it.

You don't have to have all the answers. You don't have to be OK. All you need is to take the first step: to listen, to look closer, and to begin. The rest will follow.

Chapter 1: The Zero-Point of Discord
Section A: Fractured Beginnings

The Arrival of Chaos

Chaos feels like an ambush. One moment, the ground beneath you seems steady, familiar, reliable. The next, everything cracks apart, and the stability you took for granted dissolves into uncertainty. It doesn't just disturb your plans or your sense of direction—it unsettles something deeper, something foundational. Chaos doesn't ask permission. It doesn't arrive on a convenient schedule. It crashes into your life with all the subtlety of breaking glass, leaving you standing amidst the shards, unsure where to begin.

In those moments, it's hard not to feel betrayed. Why now? Why me? It's easy to believe that chaos is an attack, something the universe has unleashed specifically to upend you. But chaos isn't personal. It doesn't choose victims or operate with malice. It arises wherever alignment has been lost, wherever trust has been fractured, wherever clarity has been overtaken by ambiguity. It isn't an enemy—it's a signal. Chaos doesn't attack—it reveals.

At first, chaos feels sudden. It seems to erupt out of nowhere, catching you completely off guard. But chaos is rarely as abrupt as it appears. It is the culmination of smaller fractures left unattended. A strained relationship ignored until the tension snaps. A series of compromises that pull you further from your values. A creeping disconnection from yourself that goes unnoticed until it manifests as crisis. Chaos builds in the shadows, widening the cracks you didn't want to look at until they can no longer be ignored.

This realization can feel overwhelming. To see chaos as

cumulative is to confront the uncomfortable truth that it didn't come from nowhere—it came from somewhere. It came from the spaces where you've been out of alignment, the places where you've avoided what felt too difficult to face. Chaos holds up a mirror, reflecting back not just the fractures, but the choices and patterns that led to them. It forces you to see what has been left unresolved.

The temptation is to look away, to avert your gaze from what the mirror shows you. Chaos is uncomfortable, and your instincts may urge you to distract yourself, to cover over the brokenness, to find something quick and temporary to patch the cracks. But chaos doesn't allow itself to be dismissed so easily. It doesn't demand immediate solutions, but it does demand attention. It asks you to pause, to notice, to sit with what feels unresolvable. Not to blame yourself, not to punish yourself, but to understand.

Sitting with chaos is not about fixing it all at once. It's about listening to what it's telling you. Chaos doesn't arrive to punish you—it arrives to guide you. It points to the spaces that need repair, the relationships that need care, the values that need realignment. It isn't here to destroy—it's here to teach. And what it teaches is not always easy to accept. It teaches patience when you want action. It teaches presence when you want escape. It teaches you to see what is, even when what is feels unbearable.

This is the zero-point of discord: the moment when everything feels broken, and yet, within that brokenness, something begins. This is not the end of your story. It is the space where the story shifts, where the fractures reveal something you couldn't see before. Chaos doesn't offer answers, but it does offer questions. It doesn't promise resolution, but it creates the conditions for it. If you can sit with the discomfort, if you can resist the urge to cover or fix or flee, you can begin to see the possibilities hidden in the fractures.

Chaos isn't easy. It isn't gentle. But it is transformative. To face chaos is to face what has been left unspoken, unresolved, unnoticed. To sit with it is to take the first step toward something new. It won't happen all at once, and it won't happen without discomfort. But it will happen. Chaos is not the end—it is the beginning. And from the beginning, anything is possible.

The Reflection in the Cracks

To stand in the aftermath of chaos is to face a reflection you didn't ask for. The cracks it leaves behind act as a mirror, showing you not only what has broken, but also the parts of yourself and your life that led to this moment. It's uncomfortable to look. It's easier to focus on the mess, to rush toward cleaning it up, to patch the surface and move on. But chaos isn't asking for a quick fix—it's asking for your attention.

In the cracks, there are stories. Each one tells of a fracture that grew quietly, unnoticed, until it couldn't be ignored. Perhaps it's a compromise you made again and again, believing it was small enough not to matter. Or a silence you kept because speaking would have felt too risky. Maybe it's a distance that slowly widened until you could no longer see the person—or the part of yourself—on the other side. Chaos doesn't create these fractures; it reveals them.

This is why chaos feels so personal. It forces you to confront not just the external circumstances, but the internal patterns that shaped them. It holds up a mirror to the choices, the fears, and the avoidances that brought you here. It whispers, *Look closer.* It is not judging you—it is guiding you. And the closer you look, the more you begin to see.

At first, all you see is the brokenness. The jagged edges, the gaps where there used to be connection, the pieces that no longer seem to fit. But as you sit with the cracks, as you resist the urge to cover them, something shifts. You begin to notice the spaces between them—the spaces where something new might take root. The cracks are not just the result of what has been lost; they are the openings through which transformation begins.

This isn't an easy realization. It's far simpler to blame the chaos itself, to see it as an outside force that disrupted what was otherwise fine. But chaos doesn't appear in a vacuum. It emerges from the spaces where alignment has been missing. And when you begin to see it this way, it stops being something to escape and starts being something to understand.

Chaos invites you to see the whole picture—not just the cracks, but the patterns they reveal. It asks you to trace the fractures back to their origins, to understand where things began to splinter. It's not about finding fault or assigning blame. It's about learning. What have the cracks taught you about what matters? What have they shown you about what you need, about what you've been avoiding, about what you can no longer ignore?

This reflection isn't about judgment. It's about clarity. Chaos doesn't demand perfection—it asks for presence. It asks you to sit with the discomfort of what is, so that you can begin to imagine what could be. The cracks are not the end of the story. They are the beginning of something new.

Transformation starts here, in the stillness, in the moment when you stop running from the fractures and start listening to them. Chaos is the signal. The cracks are the map. And the work of realignment begins not when the pieces are forced back together, but when you allow yourself to see the spaces between them. Those spaces are where growth happens. Those spaces are where clarity begins.

You don't have to have all the answers. You don't have to know what the next step looks like. You only have to begin. And beginning starts with looking—not away, but closer. This is the reflection in the cracks. It's uncomfortable, yes. But it's also where the light gets in.

Section B: The Starting Void
The Weight of Uncertainty

When chaos arrives, it leaves behind a void—a space where the structures you relied on no longer hold, where the answers you thought you had dissolve into uncertainty. This void is not empty. It is heavy, pressing, filled with everything unresolved. It holds the weight of unanswered questions, of fears too big to name, of emotions too tangled to unravel. The void is not absence—it is presence. It is the fullness of everything left undone, unspoken, unacknowledged.

At first, the void feels unbearable. It looms, vast and formless, like a shadow that stretches across everything you see. You may try to avoid it, distracting yourself with busyness or searching for quick solutions to fill the emptiness. Or you may find yourself sinking into it, overwhelmed by its scale, its depth, its silence. But the void cannot be avoided forever. It is not a problem to solve or a space to escape. It is a threshold. And thresholds are meant to be crossed.

The void isn't asking you to fill it. It's asking you to sit with it. To feel its weight, to notice its shape, to listen to what rises within it. The void is where the things we avoid gather, waiting to be named. It holds the fears we don't want to face, the truths we don't want to admit, the possibilities we don't yet know how to see. It feels overwhelming because it is unfamiliar, and what is unfamiliar always feels infinite. But the void is not infinite. It only feels that way because we haven't explored its edges.

Sitting with the void is an act of courage. It means resisting the urge to fix, to escape, to explain. It means allowing yourself to feel the weight of uncertainty without rushing to lighten it. The void asks you to pause, to wait, to listen—not because it has answers to give, but because it holds the space where answers can begin to form.

This stillness is uncomfortable. The urge to act, to solve, to resolve is strong, especially when everything feels unresolved. But the void cannot be rushed. It moves at the pace of your willingness to be present with it. The more you resist, the heavier it feels. The more you lean in, the clearer its shape becomes. Slowly, the formlessness gives way to form. The overwhelming vastness begins to shrink. The edges come into focus. And within those edges, you begin to see the outlines of something new.

The void is not your enemy. It is not a punishment. It is a space of potential. It holds everything unresolved, yes, but it also holds everything possible. To step into the void is to step into the space where transformation begins. It is not about fixing or filling—it is about listening and creating. The void doesn't demand solutions; it invites you to make room for what's next.

Naming the Shadows

The void is not silent. It whispers, it hums, it echoes with the fragments of things we've avoided, the fears and uncertainties we've tried to suppress. These shadows within the void are not new; they've always been there, lingering at the edges of our awareness, waiting for us to notice them. Chaos simply clears the way, making their presence impossible to ignore.

At first, these shadows feel overwhelming, like a cacophony of unresolved emotions and unanswered questions all vying for attention at once. Fear of failure. Guilt for mistakes. Regret for what might have been. The weight of expectations unmet. These shadows speak loudly because they've been unheard for so long. And yet, within the noise, there is meaning. Each shadow holds a piece of the truth we need to find clarity and move forward.

Naming the shadows is an act of self-recognition. It means looking into the void and saying, *Yes, I see you. I hear you. I know you are here.* It's not about judgment or justification; it's about acknowledgment. The shadows are not there to hurt you —they are there to guide you. Each one is a signal, pointing to a part of yourself or your experience that needs attention, care, or understanding.

But naming the shadows takes courage. It asks you to stand still in the void, to resist the urge to run or hide, and to let the whispers rise to the surface. It asks you to ask yourself questions you may not want to answer. What am I afraid of losing? What am I holding onto that no longer serves me? What part of myself have I hidden because I thought it wasn't enough? The answers may be difficult, but they are also liberating. To name the shadows is to begin to know them, and to know them is to begin to integrate them.

The void becomes less intimidating as its shadows take shape. The vast, overwhelming space begins to feel smaller, more manageable. Its contours come into focus. What once seemed infinite is revealed to have edges, boundaries, limits. And within those boundaries, you begin to find the possibility of creating something new. The shadows lose their power when they are named, when they are brought into the light of your attention. They become not obstacles, but teachers.

This doesn't mean the void becomes comfortable. Sitting with it is still difficult, and the shadows will still challenge you. But their challenge is a gift. They ask you to confront the parts of yourself that you've left in the dark and to see those parts not as flaws, but as pieces of the whole. The void is where clarity begins—not because it provides answers, but because it creates the space where answers can emerge.

Naming the shadows is not a single act; it is a process. It takes time, patience, and a willingness to stay present with what feels unresolved. But with each shadow named, the void becomes less about what's missing and more about what's possible. It is no longer a place of absence, but a place of presence—a space where transformation begins.

The void is not your enemy. The shadows are not your failures. They are your guides, your signals, your opportunities to grow. And as you name them, as you learn to sit with them, you begin to see the light that was always there, waiting in the dark.

Chapter 2: The Noise of Being
Section A: Endless Input

Overwhelmed by the Stream

Life is loud. It hums, buzzes, and shouts, filling every moment with demands for attention. Notifications, responsibilities, expectations—they all pile on, creating a relentless stream of input. There is always something more: another task, another message, another reminder of what hasn't been done or what needs to be done better. The noise is endless, and in its endlessness, it drowns out everything else.

This constant flood of input doesn't just occupy your mind—it fragments it. Your thoughts, emotions, and focus are pulled in so many directions that they begin to lose coherence. You find yourself circling the same worries, the same doubts, the same unfinished lists, unable to focus long enough to resolve any of them. It's not that you're doing too much; it's that too much is being asked of you, all at once, all the time.

The noise is deceptive. It feels productive, like motion, like engagement. But it's not. It's static. It keeps you stuck in patterns of reaction and distraction, filling your time with activity that lacks meaning. The more you try to keep up, the further you feel from clarity. And the more you let the noise dictate your days, the more it begins to feel like life itself.

The noise is not just external—it's internal too. The stream of thoughts running through your mind, the self-doubt, the worry, the rumination on past mistakes or future fears—they all add to the hum. It's not just the emails or the deadlines or the headlines; it's the way you carry them, the way they echo inside you long after the moment has passed. The noise isn't just what's around you; it's what's within you, amplifying every doubt, every fear, every unfinished thought.

This endless input is exhausting, but it's also numbing. It distracts you from the things that matter most—not because you don't care about them, but because the noise is so constant that it becomes all you can hear. It becomes the default, the baseline, and in its constancy, it drowns out the signals that could guide you toward clarity and connection.

To live in the noise is to live in a state of near-constant overwhelm. It leaves no space for reflection, for meaning, for being. It pulls you away from yourself, from others, from the things that truly matter. But the noise is not invincible. It can be quieted—not silenced completely, but quieted enough for the signals to come through.

Quieting the noise begins with noticing it. Noticing how it pulls you, how it fragments you, how it keeps you circling the same thoughts and patterns. Noticing where it comes from—not just the sources around you, but the echoes within you. The noise isn't just something that happens to you; it's something you can begin to understand, and in understanding, you can begin to change.

Living in the Static

The noise doesn't just surround you—it embeds itself within you. It becomes so constant, so pervasive, that you stop noticing it for what it is. It feels like life itself, like the natural state of being. But living in the static is not living. It's circling, endlessly, through distractions, worries, and unfinished tasks that keep pulling you away from yourself.

In the static, everything feels urgent. Every ping, every notification, every thought seems to demand immediate attention. But the urgency is an illusion. The noise tricks you into believing that you must respond to everything, that every task must be done, that every distraction must be followed. And in this endless reaction, the things that truly matter—the things that ground you, that connect you, that give your life meaning—fade into the background.

The static creates a kind of paralysis. It keeps you busy, but not productive. It fills your time, but not your soul. It gives you the sense of doing something without the satisfaction of having done anything. It fragments your attention, leaving you unable to focus long enough to find clarity. And in its grip, it feels inescapable.

But the static is not invincible. It feels all-encompassing because it thrives on being unnoticed, on blending into the background until it feels like the air you breathe. The first step in quieting it is to notice it, to call it out for what it is: noise. It's the static that keeps you circling the same patterns. It's the static that makes it hard to hear your own thoughts. And it's the static that can be challenged.

To live in the static is to live disconnected—from yourself, from others, from the signals that matter most. But the static is not life—it's interference. Beneath it, there is clarity waiting to be heard. Beneath it, there is meaning waiting to be found. Quieting the static isn't about silencing everything—it's about finding the signals beneath the noise.

This isn't an instant process. The static has been with you for so long that it feels like part of you, and it won't quiet itself overnight. But each time you notice it, each time you choose to step back from its pull, you create a little more space for clarity. You begin to hear the signals, faint at first but growing stronger, guiding you back to what truly matters.

Living in the static doesn't have to be permanent. It is a state, not a sentence. And the more you learn to notice it, to name it, to challenge it, the less power it holds over you. The static may always be there, humming in the background, but it doesn't have to define your days. Beneath the noise, there is a quieter rhythm, a truer voice. And when you begin to hear it, you begin to find yourself again.

Section B: Paralysis in Chaos
The Weight of Too Much

Choice is supposed to feel like power. The more options you have, the more freedom you're told you have to shape your own life. But when the choices pile too high, when every path forward feels equally pressing, equally urgent, equally risky, freedom transforms into burden. You're no longer steering your life—you're stalled at the intersection, staring at the endless possibilities with no sense of where to begin. Every option demands attention, and every decision feels like a gamble.

This is how paralysis begins—not with a dramatic moment, but with a quiet pause that stretches longer and longer. It starts with hesitation: a moment to weigh your options, to choose carefully. But the pause grows heavy. The questions multiply. What if I choose wrong? What if I fail? What if this decision shuts down something I don't even know I'll need later? The pressure builds, turning what should be a step forward into an immovable wall.

Paralysis isn't just indecision—it's the stories we attach to our choices. We freeze because the stakes feel impossibly high. We tell ourselves that this one decision will define everything that follows. And when every option feels like a potential mistake, doing nothing feels safer than doing something. But this isn't safety. It's stagnation.

The weight of too much isn't just about the choices themselves—it's about what they represent. Each one feels tied to your identity, your future, your worth. The longer you wait, the heavier that weight becomes, until even the smallest step feels impossible. Paralysis convinces you that staying still is the best option, but the longer you stay, the harder it is to move. The weight doesn't just grow—it roots itself.

Paralysis thrives in the space between fear and motion. It thrives on the illusion that doing nothing is neutral, that avoiding a choice is somehow safer than making one. But in reality, inaction is a choice of its own, and it comes with its own costs. The longer you stay in the stillness, the more it controls you. The longer you wait to move, the heavier the weight of too much becomes.

The path out of paralysis doesn't start with clarity. It doesn't start with knowing the perfect choice or having a perfect plan. It starts with motion. It starts with a step. Any step. Even the smallest motion disrupts the stillness that keeps you frozen. Even the smallest shift begins to lighten the weight. You don't need to know the destination to start moving. You just need to remember that paralysis isn't permanent. The weight is not immovable. It changes when you change.

Breaking the Freeze

Paralysis isn't just about the weight of choices—it's about the stories we tell ourselves about those choices. We freeze because we believe that every decision must be perfect, that every path forward must lead directly to success or fulfillment. We convince ourselves that the stakes are impossibly high, that any mistake will be catastrophic, irreversible. And so, we stay still, caught in the freeze, unable to move in any direction for fear that it might be the wrong one.

Breaking the freeze means challenging these stories. It means shifting the way you think about choices, about risk, about motion itself. The freeze isn't just about indecision—it's about fear. The fear of failure. The fear of regret. The fear that no matter what you choose, it won't be enough. These fears don't disappear on their own. They linger, feeding the stillness, keeping you stuck in the same loop of hesitation. But fear is not immovable. It changes when you change.

To break the freeze, you don't need a perfect plan or a grand gesture. You need a step. One small step, no matter how insignificant it seems. Choose one thing to move toward—not because it's the "right" thing, but because it's something. Motion is what disrupts the freeze, not clarity. Clarity comes later, after the stillness has been broken, after the momentum has begun.

But even small steps can feel impossible when you're frozen. That's because the freeze convinces you that the stakes are higher than they are. It tells you that every decision is permanent, that every move is irreversible. But most decisions are not final. Most paths can be adjusted. Most mistakes can be corrected. The freeze thrives on the illusion of permanence, but breaking it requires remembering that very few choices in life are truly fixed.

The first step may feel small, even trivial. It may feel like it doesn't matter. But it does. The act of moving—even in the smallest way —creates momentum. And momentum creates space. It shifts the perspective, softens the edges of the fears that kept you frozen, and allows you to see the next step, and then the next. Breaking the freeze is not about solving everything at once—it's about remembering that you can move.

You won't always know where the first step will lead. That's part of what makes it hard. But the act of stepping forward is what begins to break the hold of paralysis. The stillness loses its power when you challenge it, when you remind yourself that motion is possible, even if you don't have all the answers. You don't have to know the whole path to take the first step. And once you've taken it, the next step becomes clearer.

The freeze thrives on fear, but fear thrives on inaction. Breaking the freeze isn't about erasing the fear—it's about moving through it. It's about choosing to act, even when the outcome is uncertain. It's about remembering that stillness is not safety, and that even the smallest motion is a victory.

Chapter 3: Fragments of the Self
Section A: Broken Mirrors

Shattered Reflections

When you look at yourself, what do you see? Is it a single, cohesive image—a sense of wholeness and clarity? Or is it fragments? A thousand scattered reflections, each one capturing a piece of who you think you are, but none of them adding up to a complete picture. For many of us, it's the latter. The mirror we hold up to ourselves is cracked, fractured, distorted by expectations, doubts, and unresolved tensions. We see pieces of ourselves, but not the whole.

These fractures don't happen all at once. They appear slowly, over time, widening with each unanswered question, each unspoken fear, each unresolved moment. A piece of yourself becomes hidden because someone told you it wasn't good enough. Another piece warps because you believed you needed to be something you weren't. Over time, the mirror that once reflected your true self becomes fragmented, and the person you see is no longer someone you recognize.

This fragmentation feels like disconnection. You feel distant from yourself, unsure of who you are or who you're supposed to be. It's as though the pieces of your identity are scattered across a room, and no matter how hard you try to gather them, some remain out of reach. The more you focus on what's missing, the more broken the image appears.

But the cracks in the mirror are not flaws—they are clues. They show you where the dissonance lies, where the alignment is missing, where the work of understanding needs to begin. Each fragment holds a piece of your story, a piece of truth about what you value, what you fear, and what you need. To see yourself clearly again, you don't need to erase the cracks—you need to learn from them.

This process begins with curiosity. What do the fractures in your reflection tell you? What stories do they hold? What parts of yourself have been hidden, and why? The cracks may feel like failures, but they are opportunities. They invite you to look closer, to ask questions, to explore the parts of yourself that you've been avoiding. The broken mirror isn't here to punish you—it's here to guide you.

Reassembling the mirror doesn't mean forcing the pieces back together. It means understanding what each piece represents and how it fits into the whole. It means accepting that the cracks are part of the story, part of what makes you human. The reflection will never be perfect, but it can be honest. And honesty is where clarity begins.

Piecing It Together

The fragments of the mirror don't lie—they reveal. Each shard reflects a moment, a truth, a piece of yourself that has been shaped by experience. Some pieces are sharp and jagged, cutting to the touch. Others are smooth, softened by time, their edges worn down by reflection and acceptance. Together, they form a mosaic of who you are, but only if you're willing to look at them closely, to pick them up one by one, and begin to understand their place in the whole.

To piece the mirror together, you first have to accept that it will never be perfect. It will never return to the seamless reflection it once was—or the one you imagined it should be. And that's OK. The goal isn't perfection; it's coherence. It's about seeing the fragments not as failures, but as chapters in your story, each one carrying its own meaning, its own lesson, its own place in the larger picture.

Some fragments will reflect the parts of yourself you're proud of —the times you acted with courage, the moments when you felt aligned with your values, the relationships where you felt deeply connected. These pieces are easier to hold, easier to accept. But others will reflect the parts of yourself you'd rather not see—the moments of fear, the mistakes, the relationships where trust was broken, the dreams that were left behind. These pieces are harder to face, but they are no less important.

When you start to place the pieces together, the cracks will still show. The lines between the fragments won't disappear. But those lines don't diminish the reflection—they give it depth. They show where healing has happened, where growth has occurred, where understanding has deepened. The cracks are not flaws; they are evidence of your resilience, your willingness to keep looking, your commitment to knowing yourself fully.

Piecing the mirror together is not about erasing the past— it's about integrating it. It's about taking the parts of yourself that feel disconnected and bringing them into alignment. It's about recognizing that wholeness doesn't mean flawless; it means honest. The mirror may still be fractured, but it will be yours—reflecting not just who you are, but who you're becoming.

To live with a fractured mirror is to live with truth. It's to accept that you are not one thing, but many. It's to see yourself as dynamic, evolving, layered. And as you piece the fragments together, you begin to see not just the cracks, but the light that shines through them. The mirror becomes less about what's broken and more about what's possible.

The work of piecing yourself together is never finished. There will always be new cracks, new fractures, new moments when the reflection feels unclear. But with each piece you examine, with each fragment you integrate, you strengthen the whole. You create a reflection that is not static, but alive—capable of holding the full spectrum of your humanity.

Section B: The Disaffected Youth
Inheriting the Fractures

Youth is supposed to be a time of possibility. The world feels open, horizons seem endless, and life holds the promise of something extraordinary just beyond reach. But for many, that promise feels hollow. Instead of possibility, youth becomes a time of dissonance —of clashing expectations, unspoken contradictions, and the weight of a world that feels broken before you've even had a chance to understand it.

For the disaffected youth, this fracture begins early. They inherit not just the world as it is, but the unresolved tensions of those who came before them. Generational conflicts, systemic inequities, environmental crises—these are the legacies passed down, often without acknowledgment or preparation. The world they are told to step into feels contradictory: a place where they are told to dream big, yet are handed systems that seem designed to stifle those dreams.

This dissonance creates a profound sense of frustration, one that is often mistaken for rebellion or apathy. But beneath that frustration is something deeper: a desire for clarity, for authenticity, for a world that makes sense. The disaffected youth are not rejecting the world because they don't care—they are rejecting it because they care too much. They see the fractures more clearly than most, and they are unwilling to accept them as inevitable.

But the weight of those fractures can be overwhelming. It feels like being handed a puzzle with pieces missing, and no picture to guide you. You try to make sense of what's in front of you, but nothing fits, and the harder you try, the more disconnected you feel. This is the disaffection of youth—not a failure of character, but a response to a world that has handed you its broken pieces without showing you how to put them together.

The disaffected youth carry both a burden and a potential. The burden is the dissonance they've inherited, the fractures they've been asked to live within. The potential is the clarity they can bring to those fractures, the courage to question, to challenge, to imagine something better. They see the cracks not as failures, but as opportunities for change.

The Spark of Discontent

Disaffection is often misunderstood. It's seen as laziness, as rebellion for rebellion's sake, as an unwillingness to engage with the world in a productive way. But disaffection isn't apathy—it's a spark. It's the response of someone who sees the world's fractures too clearly to pretend they aren't there. It's the frustration of being asked to live within systems that feel broken, to play by rules that make no sense, to dream within limits that have already been set.

For the disaffected youth, this spark comes from a deep desire for authenticity, for meaning, for something more. They don't want to reject the world—they want to reshape it. They want a world that aligns with their values, that reflects their ideals, that feels worthy of the dreams they've been told to pursue. But when those dreams clash with the reality they see, the result is disconnection, frustration, and often, despair.

This disconnection doesn't come from a lack of care—it comes from caring too much. It's the dissonance between what they believe the world could be and what it is. It's the gap between the stories they've been told about success, fulfillment, and happiness, and the reality of systems that seem designed to exclude, exploit, or oppress. The disaffected youth are not indifferent—they are paying attention. And what they see doesn't align with what they've been told.

But discontent is not the end of the story. It's the beginning. Discontent is the spark that challenges the status quo, that asks the uncomfortable questions, that imagines new possibilities. It's the energy that drives movements, innovations, and revolutions. The disaffected youth may feel disconnected, but that disconnection holds the potential for transformation.

To hold this spark is to hold both frustration and hope. It's to see the fractures in the world and to believe that they can be mended —not with quick fixes or superficial solutions, but with deeper, systemic change. The spark of discontent isn't about tearing everything down—it's about creating the space for something better to emerge.

The challenge for the disaffected youth is to keep that spark alive without letting it burn them out. Frustration can be fuel, but it can also consume. The key is to channel that energy into action, into creativity, into connection. It's about finding others who see the same fractures, who feel the same dissonance, and who share the same desire for change. Together, the spark becomes a flame, and the flame becomes a light.

Disaffection isn't a failure—it's a signal. It's the beginning of a journey, not the end of one. And for those who carry it, the question isn't whether the world can be fixed—it's how they will choose to shape the world they've inherited.

Chapter 4: The Pessimism of Age
Section A: Time's Erosion

The Weight of Disappointment

Time has a way of softening sharp edges, of smoothing the surfaces of our memories until they feel manageable, even comforting. But time also layers itself upon us, each year leaving its mark. Dreams deferred, expectations unmet, and moments lost to hesitation or regret—these aren't isolated events. They settle into us, becoming part of the weight we carry.

As we age, this weight can feel heavier. It's not that life stops offering possibility, but the accumulation of disappointments begins to obscure those possibilities. The idealism of youth fades, replaced by the steady erosion of what once seemed certain. Where we once believed in endless potential, we now see limits— limits of time, of energy, of what feels achievable. It's not that the world has grown smaller; it's that we've grown more aware of its constraints.

The weight of disappointment is cumulative. A single missed opportunity feels manageable, even forgettable. But over time, the pattern becomes harder to ignore. It's not just about what was lost —it's about the fear that those losses define what remains. You begin to wonder if the best moments have already passed, if the dreams you once held have quietly expired without you noticing.

This is the erosion of time—the slow wearing away of wonder, the quiet narrowing of horizons. It's not dramatic, and it doesn't happen all at once. It's subtle, like sediment settling at the bottom of a river, clouding the waters and making it harder to see what lies ahead. And as the sediment builds, it creates a filter through which we view the world. Where we once saw endless possibility, we now see barriers. Where we once saw potential, we now see doubt.

But the erosion of time is not absolute. Beneath the sediment, the river still flows. The dreams you once held, the wonder you once felt—they haven't disappeared. They've been buried, obscured by the weight of years, but they are still there, waiting to be uncovered. Time doesn't just take—it transforms. And what feels like an end can become a beginning, if you're willing to sift through the layers.

To confront the weight of disappointment is to confront the stories you've told yourself about what those disappointments mean. It's to challenge the narrative that what was lost defines what's possible. Time's erosion is real, but it doesn't have to be permanent. Beneath the layers of what was, there is still the possibility of what could be.

Beneath the Sediment

Time's erosion doesn't just cloud the present—it reshapes how we view the past. The disappointments we've experienced, the opportunities we missed, the relationships that ended before they began to flourish—all of these moments settle into us, becoming a lens through which we see the world. The sediment doesn't just obscure—it alters, reframing our memories, coloring them with a subtle shade of regret, and making it harder to believe that the future could hold something different.

This accumulation creates a paradox. As we age, we gain perspective, experience, and wisdom—tools that should make us better equipped to navigate life. And yet, these same tools often come with the weight of everything we've lived through, everything that didn't go as we hoped. It's not that we stop dreaming—it's that our dreams feel further away, harder to justify, easier to dismiss as unrealistic.

The sediment of time is insidious because it convinces us that what we've lost defines us more than what we still have. It tells us that the barriers we see are unmovable, that the disappointments we've experienced are inevitable, that the best moments are behind us. But this narrative is not the whole truth. The sediment doesn't erase what lies beneath it—it only obscures it. And just as rivers run deep beneath layers of silt, so too does your capacity for wonder, for curiosity, for possibility.

Beneath the sediment, the river still flows. The dreams you once held, the ideals you believed in, the joy you felt—they haven't disappeared. They've been buried, yes, but they are still there, waiting for you to uncover them. Time's erosion doesn't have to be the end of wonder. It can be the beginning of rediscovery.

Rediscovering what lies beneath the sediment isn't about trying to relive the past. It's about recognizing that what you thought was lost has only been transformed. The dreams you held may not look the same as they once did, but that doesn't mean they've disappeared. They've evolved, just as you have. The wonder you once felt may feel buried, but it's still there, waiting for you to reach for it.

To sift through the sediment is to ask yourself what you've let go of—not because it was unimportant, but because life demanded it. It's to ask whether those things are truly gone or if they've simply been waiting for you to look beneath the surface. The barriers you see now may not be as solid as they seem. They may be markers, not walls—reminders of what you still care about, what still matters, what still has the power to move you.

Time doesn't just take—it transforms. The sediment of disappointment isn't the end of your story. It's part of it. And within that sediment are seeds of possibility, waiting to be uncovered, waiting to grow.

Section B: Replacing Wonder with Disillusionment
The Closing Horizon

When you are young, the horizon feels infinite. Possibility stretches endlessly in every direction, and the future seems like an open expanse waiting to be explored. But as the years pass, the horizon begins to narrow. The paths you didn't take grow more visible, not as possibilities but as barriers. The future starts to feel less like an open field and more like a series of closed doors.

This narrowing isn't sudden. It happens gradually, as the weight of life accumulates. Disappointments, failures, and compromises leave their mark, not just on your memories but on your sense of what is still possible. The optimism that once fueled you feels harder to access, and the world you once dreamed of building begins to feel out of reach. What you used to see as endless potential now feels like a maze with fewer and fewer exits.

But this isn't just about the world outside of you—it's also about the world within. The horizon narrows because your perspective narrows. You begin to filter everything through the lens of what you've experienced, what you've lost, what you fear might no longer be possible. Wonder doesn't disappear entirely, but it becomes harder to hold onto, harder to justify. The more you focus on what didn't work out, the harder it is to believe that anything might.

Disillusionment isn't the loss of dreams—it's the loss of faith in their possibility. It's the moment when you stop believing that the horizon holds something new, something worth reaching for. And the more this belief fades, the smaller the horizon becomes, until it feels like you're standing still, surrounded by walls instead of open space.

But horizons don't close on their own. They close because we stop walking toward them. They close because we let fear, doubt, and disappointment convince us that the barriers are real, that the potential for something new no longer exists. The truth is, the horizon is still there—it's just waiting for you to take a step toward it.

Disillusionment is not a fixed state. It feels permanent because it thrives on stillness, on the absence of movement. But the moment you begin to walk again, the horizon starts to shift. The walls you thought were unmovable start to blur. The space between you and possibility begins to grow, and with it, your sense of what might still be waiting for you.

Rekindling the Horizon

Disillusionment feels like a door closing. The things you once dreamed of, the paths you imagined walking, seem further and further out of reach. Over time, it becomes easier to believe they were never real to begin with, that they were illusions you mistook for possibilities. The optimism of youth fades, replaced by a steady refrain of *this is just how things are*. But disillusionment, like the narrowing horizon, is not permanent. It's a lens, not a truth.

The stories we tell ourselves about what's no longer possible are powerful. They shape how we see the world and what we believe it can offer. When we focus on the doors that have closed, we stop noticing the ones that are still open. When we fixate on what didn't happen, we lose sight of what still might. Disillusionment is not about the world outside of you—it's about the lens you're looking through. And lenses can be shifted.

To rekindle the horizon is not to erase the past. The disappointments, the missed opportunities, the compromises— they're real, and they matter. But they don't define what comes next. The horizon narrows not because possibility disappears, but because we stop looking for it. When we begin to shift our focus, to explore the edges of what still feels possible, the horizon begins to widen again.

This isn't about pretending everything is fine or denying the reality of what's been lost. It's about curiosity. It's about asking, *What might still be out there? What might still be waiting to be discovered, even if it looks different than I expected?* Wonder doesn't have to vanish as we age—it just changes shape. It becomes quieter, steadier, more grounded. It's no longer the boundless energy of youth, but the gentle recognition that growth is still possible, that the world is still capable of surprising you.

Rekindling the horizon is not a single act—it's a practice. It's choosing, again and again, to look beyond the barriers you've built in your mind. It's stepping toward the horizon, even when you don't know what's waiting on the other side. The act of stepping is what matters, because with each step, the horizon grows a little wider. And as it widens, so does your capacity to dream, to hope, to believe that there is still more to explore.

Disillusionment tells you that the best moments are behind you, that the possibilities have already passed. But disillusionment is just a story, and stories can be rewritten. The horizon is still there, waiting. And when you begin to walk toward it, you remind yourself that wonder was never lost—it was only waiting for you to notice it again.

Chapter 5: The Desperation of Deprivation
Section A: Scarcity's Shadow

Living Without Enough

Scarcity casts a long shadow. It stretches across every aspect of life, touching not just what we have but how we think, how we act, how we see ourselves. It's not just the absence of something—it's the feeling that what you lack defines you. Scarcity whispers that you'll never have enough, never be enough, never find enough to feel secure, connected, whole.

This isn't just about material deprivation, though that's where scarcity often begins. A lack of resources—money, food, stability—creates a constant undercurrent of worry, a baseline hum of stress that makes it hard to think beyond the next day, the next bill, the next meal. But scarcity doesn't stop with the material. It seeps into the emotional, the relational, the spiritual. It creates a mindset of insufficiency, a belief that there's always something missing, something unattainable, something just out of reach.

Scarcity doesn't just affect what we pursue—it affects how we pursue it. It convinces us to hold on tightly to what little we have, to hoard our time, our energy, our affection, believing that to give anything away is to risk losing everything. Scarcity makes generosity feel dangerous and trust feel impossible. It turns relationships into transactions, connection into competition. It isolates us, not because we want to be alone, but because we're afraid of what connection might cost.

But scarcity is deceptive. It feels all-encompassing, but it isn't absolute. It tells you that there's not enough, but it doesn't define what "enough" means. Scarcity thrives on vagueness, on the fear that the gap between what you have and what you need can never be closed. But the gap isn't as fixed as it seems. It shifts when you begin to question it, to define it, to challenge the stories scarcity tells.

To live in scarcity is to live with a constant ache, a feeling that something essential is missing. But scarcity isn't just an external condition—it's an internal mindset. It grows louder the more you listen to it, the more you let it convince you that what you lack is more important than what you have. But scarcity isn't invincible. It begins to lose its hold when you start to see it for what it is: a shadow, not the substance of your life.

The Echo Within

Scarcity doesn't just affect what you have—it shapes who you believe you are. When you live with the constant presence of "not enough," it begins to echo in your mind. It tells you that the lack isn't just external, but internal. It convinces you that scarcity isn't just something you experience, but something you embody. You begin to feel like you are what you don't have.

This echo becomes a filter, coloring everything you see. It magnifies every insecurity, every missed opportunity, every mistake. It tells you that you're falling behind, that others are moving forward, that you'll never catch up. It whispers that the resources you need—love, time, attention, stability—are not only scarce, but slipping further away with every moment. And so, you hold tighter to what little you have, believing that letting go would mean losing everything.

Scarcity doesn't just isolate you—it disconnects you from yourself. It keeps you focused on what's missing, leaving little room to appreciate what's present. It tells you that nothing is enough—not your efforts, not your achievements, not the relationships you've built. It's a voice that grows louder the more you listen to it, creating a feedback loop that reinforces its message.

But scarcity's echo, as powerful as it feels, is not the whole truth. It's a story—a story that thrives on vagueness and fear. The echo tells you what's missing, but it doesn't tell you what's possible. It convinces you that your worth is tied to what you lack, but it never asks you to define what "enough" really means. The power of the echo lies in its ability to go unchallenged. When you start to name it, to question it, to listen more closely, the echo begins to change.

The first step in quieting scarcity's echo is to notice it. To hear its whispers and recognize them for what they are: a voice, not a fact. Scarcity's power lies in its ability to keep you looking outward, searching for what's missing. But when you turn inward, when you begin to ask yourself what truly matters, the echo starts to fade. It doesn't disappear all at once, but with each moment of presence, with each act of gratitude, with each connection to yourself and others, the voice grows quieter.

Scarcity may always be a part of life, but it doesn't have to define it. The echo within is loudest when it goes unchallenged. But the more you listen to the quiet truths beneath it—the truths of what you have, of who you are, of what you can create—the less power scarcity holds. It is a shadow, not the substance. And shadows only grow smaller when you face the light.

Section B: Systems of Deprivation
Scarcity by Design

Scarcity often feels personal, like an individual burden to bear. You may think of it as the result of your own circumstances, choices, or limitations. But scarcity is rarely accidental. It is often designed—embedded in the systems we live within, perpetuated by structures that prioritize competition over connection, profit over people, and individual success over collective well-being. These systems don't just create scarcity; they thrive on it.

Consider how scarcity is woven into the fabric of society. Wages that never quite meet the cost of living. Educational opportunities that depend more on where you were born than on your potential. Healthcare that feels out of reach for too many. These are not random occurrences—they are outcomes of decisions, policies, and priorities that have been reinforced over time. Scarcity isn't just something you experience—it's something you've been handed.

These systems of deprivation operate invisibly, making scarcity feel inevitable. They create a culture where people are told to work harder, strive more, and compete endlessly for resources that are intentionally kept limited. The scarcity isn't a byproduct—it's the plan. When resources are hoarded at the top, those below are left fighting over what remains, too focused on survival to question why the system works this way.

Scarcity by design doesn't just affect material resources. It seeps into how we relate to one another, how we see ourselves, how we define success and worth. It convinces us to see each other as competitors rather than collaborators, to view generosity as risky and trust as naïve. It isolates us, not because connection isn't possible, but because the system discourages it. When you believe there isn't enough to go around, you hold tighter to what you have —and in doing so, you lose sight of the abundance that could come from sharing.

But scarcity by design can be recognized, named, and challenged. It begins with asking questions: Who benefits from this scarcity? Who suffers because of it? What would it look like to create systems that prioritize equity, connection, and sufficiency instead of endless competition? These questions don't have easy answers, but asking them shifts the focus from internal blame to systemic understanding. Scarcity isn't just your burden—it's a framework you've been asked to live within. And frameworks can change.

Challenging the Design

The systems that perpetuate scarcity feel immovable, like forces of nature—unseen, unspoken, but all-encompassing. They shape everything, from how resources are distributed to how success is measured to how worth is defined. But these systems are not natural. They were built, piece by piece, through decisions made over time. And what has been built can be rebuilt.

Challenging these systems begins with recognizing their design. Scarcity is maintained by structures that prioritize profit over people, that reward accumulation over collaboration, that measure progress not by well-being but by production. These structures thrive on competition, creating an endless race where the winners gain more than they need, and the rest are left to compete for what's left. The result isn't just inequality—it's disconnection, distrust, and despair.

But these systems don't just persist because of those who benefit from them. They persist because they convince us to uphold them. They convince us to believe in the myth of scarcity, to see resources as finite, to view others as competitors instead of collaborators. They tell us that to survive, we must compete, hoard, isolate. And in doing so, they keep us trapped within the very systems that create the scarcity we fear.

To challenge these systems is to challenge their narratives. It's to question the assumptions they ask us to accept: that there isn't enough to go around, that success is a zero-sum game, that individual achievement matters more than collective well-being. It's to ask what scarcity would look like if it were replaced with sufficiency, if competition were replaced with connection, if systems were designed not to extract but to sustain.

This isn't an easy process. The systems that perpetuate scarcity are deeply entrenched, and changing them requires both individual and collective action. But the first step is to see them clearly, to name them for what they are, and to imagine what could exist in their place. Scarcity thrives on invisibility. It loses its power when it is brought into the light.

Challenging the design of scarcity doesn't just change how resources are distributed—it changes how we relate to one another. It shifts the focus from individual survival to collective flourishing, from isolation to connection, from fear to trust. It reminds us that abundance isn't just about material wealth—it's about the relationships we build, the systems we create, the values we uphold.

Scarcity by design is not destiny. It is a choice—a choice we can unmake. And in unmaking it, we begin to create a world where sufficiency replaces scarcity, where connection replaces competition, where everyone has enough and no one is left behind.

Chapter 6: The Darkness of the World
Section A: Global Crisis

A World in Chaos

The world feels heavy. Every day, headlines echo with the same stories: climate change accelerating, inequalities widening, wars erupting, and entire communities left to grapple with systemic failures that feel too big, too entrenched to change. This isn't new —crises have always been a part of human history—but there's something about the scale and pace of today's challenges that makes them feel overwhelming, even paralyzing. It's not just the weight of one crisis—it's the way they intersect, amplify, and feed into one another, creating a constant hum of global dissonance.

When the world itself feels like it's unraveling, it's hard to know where to place your energy. How do you navigate your own challenges when the planet is literally on fire? How do you process your personal fears when millions of people are experiencing upheaval on an unimaginable scale? Global crises don't just magnify the dissonance in your own life—they make you question whether your struggles even matter in the grand scheme of things. They create a tension between the enormity of the world's problems and the immediacy of your own.

This tension isn't easy to hold. It's tempting to shut down, to turn away, to focus only on the things you can control and block out the rest. But the world's chaos doesn't disappear just because you stop looking at it. It lingers in the background, shaping your choices, your priorities, your sense of hope. Even when you try to ignore it, it finds its way in.

But the weight of global crises, as immense as it feels, is not a reason to disengage. It's a reason to refocus. These challenges, as overwhelming as they are, remind us that we are part of something larger—that our lives are connected to systems, to communities, to futures beyond our own. The chaos we see in the world is not separate from us—it reflects the dissonance within the systems we've built and the values we've upheld. And just as those systems were created, they can be changed.

A world in chaos asks not for grand solutions, but for meaningful action. It asks us to begin where we are, with what we have, in the spaces we can touch. The scale of the problems may feel beyond us, but the scale of our actions doesn't have to match. What matters is not solving everything at once—it's moving toward alignment, one step at a time.

The Weight of the Global

The chaos of the world is not something you can escape. It seeps into every part of life, a weight that settles across your shoulders even when you're focused on something else. The headlines might feel distant, the crises abstract, but they still find their way into your thoughts. They creep in during quiet moments, a whisper that asks: *What difference can you possibly make?*

This weight isn't just about the enormity of the problems—it's about the scale of your own place within them. It's hard not to feel small in the face of global crises. The world's challenges are so vast, so interconnected, that it's easy to feel powerless, like a single thread in an unraveling tapestry. What can one person do in the face of climate collapse, systemic inequality, wars that stretch across generations? The questions are overwhelming, and they invite despair.

But despair is not the only response. The weight of the global is heavy, but it is also a reminder: a reminder that you are part of something larger, that your choices and actions ripple outward in ways you may not always see. You are not disconnected from the systems that shape the world. You are a part of them, and being part of them means you have a role to play.

The enormity of global crises doesn't mean your actions are meaningless—it means they are part of a larger whole. The changes you make, the ways you align your choices with your values, may feel small, but they are significant. Every act of clarity, every step toward alignment, every effort to create connection within your sphere of influence adds to the collective movement toward change. The weight of the global isn't yours to carry alone. It's something we all share, and it is something we can only address together.

This isn't about solving everything at once. The scale of the problems doesn't require you to have all the answers—it requires you to begin. To notice where your values and your actions align. To see the places where you can act, even if those actions feel small. To remember that change isn't about perfection or grand gestures. It's about consistent, intentional steps toward something better.

The weight of the global is heavy, but it is also an invitation. It asks you to stop trying to carry everything and to start focusing on what's within your reach. It asks you to let go of the idea that you have to do it all and to embrace the idea that doing something is enough. The world is vast, yes. The challenges are immense. But the ripple of your actions matters, and together, those ripples create waves.

Section B: Magnified Chaos
The Feedback Loop

The chaos of the world doesn't just reflect your struggles—it amplifies them. It's a feedback loop, where personal dissonance makes global crises feel larger, and global crises make personal dissonance feel heavier. The frustrations you face in your own life echo in the news you consume, in the systems you navigate, in the tension you feel when the world outside mirrors the disconnection inside.

This magnification isn't an accident—it's a natural result of how intertwined the personal and the global have become. When you feel dissonance within yourself, the cracks in the world seem sharper, the chaos louder, the problems insurmountable. And when the world feels like it's falling apart, it amplifies the cracks within you, making your own struggles feel insignificant and overwhelming at the same time.

This cycle is exhausting. It leaves you feeling trapped, caught between the enormity of external crises and the weight of internal chaos. It tells you that nothing you do will ever be enough, that the problems are too big, too entrenched, too systemic to be touched by anything you might offer. And so, you freeze. You disengage. You tell yourself that it's better to look away than to face the endless loop of disconnection and despair.

But magnified chaos, as overwhelming as it feels, is also an opportunity. It reveals the connections between your inner world and the world outside. It shows you that the dissonance you feel isn't just personal—it's part of a larger pattern, a larger system, a larger story. And just as the external chaos amplifies your internal struggles, your internal clarity can ripple outward, creating small but meaningful shifts in the world around you.

Breaking the feedback loop doesn't mean ignoring the chaos or pretending it doesn't exist. It means stepping back, creating space, and asking: *What is within my reach? What is within my control?*

What can I align in my own life that might create a ripple of alignment beyond me? The feedback loop doesn't have to keep you stuck. It can become a cycle of growth, where the clarity you find within yourself helps you navigate the chaos outside.

Breaking the Cycle

Magnified chaos thrives on disconnection. It convinces you that the external and the internal are separate, that the problems of the world have no connection to your personal struggles, and that your personal struggles are too small to matter in the grand scheme of things. This illusion of separation keeps the cycle alive, feeding the sense of helplessness that comes from trying to navigate both personal and global dissonance without understanding their interdependence.

But the cycle can be broken—not by solving everything at once, but by shifting the way you relate to both the chaos around you and the chaos within. Breaking the cycle begins with acknowledging the connections. The frustration you feel in your relationships echoes in the systems of inequality you see in the world. The fear you carry about the future mirrors the uncertainty of a planet in crisis. These aren't separate struggles—they're reflections of the same patterns, the same misalignments, the same unresolved tensions.

When you start to see these connections, the chaos becomes less overwhelming. It doesn't disappear, but it begins to make more sense. You realize that the dissonance you feel isn't a flaw in you or in the world—it's a signal. It's pointing to the spaces where change is needed, where alignment is missing, where the work of understanding and transformation must begin.

Breaking the cycle also means shifting your focus. Magnified chaos thrives when you try to take on everything at once, when the enormity of the problems blinds you to what's within your reach. But clarity comes from narrowing your gaze, from identifying the small, meaningful actions that align with your values and your capacity. The scale of the problems doesn't mean your efforts are insignificant—it means they are part of something larger.

Every small act of alignment disrupts the feedback loop. Choosing to address a tension in your personal life, to speak honestly in a difficult conversation, to extend kindness where fear might have held you back—these acts ripple outward, challenging the patterns of disconnection that fuel magnified chaos. The chaos doesn't end, but it shifts. The loop becomes less about amplification and more about integration.

Breaking the cycle isn't about fixing everything. It's about remembering that the personal and the global are not separate. Your inner clarity shapes your outer actions, and your outer actions contribute to the larger systems around you. The chaos you feel may be magnified, but so is your capacity to create change, both within and beyond yourself.

Chapter 7: The Allure of the Void
Section A: Temptation of Nihilism

The Seductive Whisper

When chaos becomes too loud, too overwhelming, there's a whisper that begins to rise. It speaks softly at first, in the background of your thoughts, but its message grows stronger the longer the dissonance lingers. *What if none of this matters?* it asks. *What if nothing has meaning? Wouldn't it be easier to stop trying? To let go of the weight of caring?* This is the voice of nihilism, and it is as seductive as it is dangerous.

Nihilism offers an escape—not from the chaos, but from the pain of engaging with it. It promises that if you stop believing in meaning, in connection, in purpose, you can protect yourself from disappointment, failure, and loss. If nothing matters, then nothing can hurt. It's a logic that feels almost comforting in its simplicity. Let go, the voice says. Stop trying. Stop hoping. Stop caring.

But the comfort of nihilism is an illusion. Letting go of meaning doesn't free you from the weight of dissonance—it deepens it. When you disengage, you don't escape the chaos; you disconnect from the things that could help you navigate it. The act of giving up on meaning creates its own kind of paralysis, leaving you stuck in a void where nothing matters, nothing moves, and nothing grows.

The seduction of nihilism lies in its immediacy. It offers relief in the moment, a way to stop feeling the tension, the uncertainty, the fear. But that relief comes at a cost. The longer you stay in the void, the harder it becomes to find your way back. The void doesn't offer freedom—it offers numbness. And numbness, while it may feel safe, is not a place where life can flourish.

The temptation of nihilism is real. It's understandable. When everything feels overwhelming, the idea of disengaging can feel like the only way to protect yourself. But the void is not protection. It is a space where your fears echo louder, where the absence of meaning doesn't ease your pain but amplifies it. To resist the void is not to deny its presence—it is to recognize its whispers for what they are: an invitation to disconnect from what makes you human.

The Trap of Disengagement

The void has a way of convincing you it's safer to stay disconnected. It whispers that meaning is a burden, that hope is a liability, that the only way to protect yourself from pain is to stop engaging altogether. The trap of disengagement isn't just about giving up on the world—it's about giving up on yourself. It's about retreating so deeply into the void that you no longer remember how to step out of it.

The appeal of the void lies in its simplicity. If you don't care, you can't fail. If nothing matters, then nothing can hurt. It offers the illusion of control, a way to shield yourself from the chaos and uncertainty of life by refusing to participate in it. But the void isn't empty—it's full. Full of unanswered questions, unresolved tensions, and unspoken fears. The more you try to escape into it, the more it surrounds you, pulling you deeper into its silence.

Disengagement feels like a refuge, but it's a prison. It isolates you, cutting you off from the connections, the passions, the growth that give life its meaning. The absence of hope doesn't protect you from pain—it magnifies it, because it takes away the tools you need to move through it. The longer you stay in the void, the more it convinces you that leaving isn't possible, that the numbness is all that remains.

But the void, as consuming as it feels, is not infinite. It thrives on inaction, on the absence of movement. The trap of disengagement isn't about the void itself—it's about the stories you tell yourself while you're in it. *This is safer. This is easier. This is the only option left.* These stories keep you stuck, but they are not the truth. The truth is that the void loses its power the moment you begin to name it, to question it, to see it for what it is: a space, not a sentence.

To step out of the void doesn't mean solving everything at once. It doesn't mean replacing despair with instant hope or chaos with immediate clarity. It means choosing to engage, even in small ways. It means reaching for something, anything, that reconnects you to the world outside the void. A conversation. A walk. A moment of curiosity. The void convinces you that meaning is unreachable, but the act of reaching is what begins to change everything.

Disengagement is the void's greatest weapon, but connection is its antidote. Every small act of engagement—every step toward connection, every choice to care, every moment of openness—weakens the hold of the void. It reminds you that life isn't about perfection or certainty—it's about motion, about trying, about being present with what is, even when it feels overwhelming.

The trap of disengagement tells you that staying in the void is easier than stepping out. But the void doesn't offer ease—it offers emptiness. To resist it is not to fight it, but to reach beyond it, to remember that the whisper of nihilism is not a truth—it's a shadow. And shadows, no matter how heavy they feel, are not the substance of your life.

Section B: Descent into Meaninglessness
The Pull of the Abyss

The void doesn't arrive all at once. It begins as a whisper, a quiet tug at the edges of your thoughts. *What if nothing matters? What if all this effort is pointless?* These questions start small, almost imperceptible, but they grow with every moment of dissonance, every failure, every disappointment. Before you realize it, the whisper becomes a pull, and the pull becomes a plunge.

The descent into meaninglessness feels like relief at first. Letting go of meaning seems to lift the weight of expectations, the pressure to perform, the fear of failure. If nothing matters, then nothing can disappoint you. If nothing matters, then you don't have to try, to risk, to care. The void convinces you that disengagement is freedom, that detachment is strength. But this freedom is hollow, and this strength is fragile.

The deeper you sink into the void, the more its pull intensifies. It tells you that meaning is a lie, that hope is for the naïve, that connection is a trap. It whispers that the numbness you feel is safety, that the emptiness is better than the pain. But the void doesn't protect you—it isolates you. It cuts you off from the very things that make life worth living: connection, curiosity, growth.

The pull of the void thrives on inertia. The longer you stay in its grip, the harder it feels to climb out. It convinces you that moving forward is pointless, that reaching out is futile, that trying again will only lead to more disappointment. But these whispers are not truths—they are echoes of your fear, your pain, your exhaustion. They are not permanent, and they are not you.

The descent into meaninglessness is not inevitable. The void may pull at you, but you are not powerless. The first step in resisting its pull is to notice it, to name it, to recognize it for what it is: a voice, not a fact. The void tells you that nothing matters, but the act of noticing its whispers is proof that you still care, that something still matters to you. And that spark, no matter how small, is where the climb begins.

The Climb Out

The void doesn't just pull you in—it builds walls around you. As you sink deeper, the world outside begins to feel distant, almost unreachable. The numbness that once felt protective becomes suffocating. You no longer feel the pain of dissonance, but you also no longer feel the warmth of connection, the spark of curiosity, the drive to grow. The void convinces you that this stillness is better than struggle, that staying here, in this silent, weightless place, is easier than facing what lies beyond it.

But the void isn't a sanctuary—it's a stasis. It offers no paths forward, no bridges to understanding, no doors to possibility. It keeps you circling the same doubts, the same fears, the same unanswered questions, convincing you that movement is impossible and that stillness is your only option. The longer you remain, the harder it feels to imagine leaving. The walls grow higher, the silence deeper, the numbness heavier.

To climb out of the void is not to deny its existence—it is to see it for what it is. The void is not infinite; it only feels that way because you've stopped moving. Its walls are not solid; they are made of the stories you've told yourself about what is and isn't possible. *Nothing matters. I can't do this. I'll never get it right.* These stories build the walls higher, make the silence louder, keep the numbness in place. But walls made of stories can be dismantled, one thought at a time.

The climb out begins with a single question: *What if something does matter?* The void tells you that nothing is worth the effort, that no path leads anywhere meaningful, but this question challenges that narrative. It doesn't ask you to know what matters —it simply invites you to consider the possibility. And that possibility is a crack in the wall, a faint light in the darkness, a reminder that the numbness isn't the whole truth.

The void thrives on inaction, on the belief that movement is impossible. But the act of questioning it—the act of imagining something beyond it—is a form of motion. It disrupts the stasis, creates a space where hope can begin to take root, even if it's just a tiny seed. To climb out of the void doesn't mean leaping to clarity or joy; it means choosing one small action, one moment of engagement, one step toward connection.

That step might feel insignificant. It might be reaching out to a friend, reading a single sentence that sparks curiosity, or simply taking a breath and acknowledging the weight of the void without judgment. The act of stepping, no matter how small, is what matters. Each step creates momentum, and with momentum, the walls of the void begin to shift. They become less imposing, less permanent. The climb doesn't have to be perfect—it just has to begin.

The void convinces you that it is the only option, that leaving it is too hard, too uncertain, too risky. But the risk isn't in climbing out —the risk is in staying. The longer you remain, the more the void takes from you: your curiosity, your connection, your sense of self. The climb is difficult, yes, but it is also necessary. Each small act of engagement is a declaration: *I am still here. I still care. I am still reaching.*

The climb out of the void is not about finding instant clarity or erasing the dissonance that brought you here. It's about rediscovering the things that matter—not all at once, but one at a time. It's about remembering that meaning isn't something you find; it's something you create. The void may surround you now, but it doesn't define you. You are not its prisoner. The climb is within you, and every step is a step toward becoming more of who you are.

Chapter 8: The Tyranny of Reaction
Section A: Emotions Out of Control

The Grip of Fear and Anger

When the world feels like too much—when dissonance overwhelms and chaos surrounds—it's easy to let emotions take control. Fear surges in, warning you of dangers you can't quite name. Anger flares up, demanding justice for wrongs you can't always articulate. These emotions are powerful, visceral, and immediate. They feel like the only forces you can trust in a moment of uncertainty. But when fear and anger are in control, they don't guide you toward clarity—they push you further into the chaos.

Fear grips tightly, shrinking your perspective until all you can see are the threats around you. It whispers that you are unsafe, unprepared, incapable. Its urgency pulls your attention away from possibilities, away from solutions, away from connection. It narrows your world to a single question: *How do I survive?* And in its grip, even the simplest actions feel overwhelming.

Anger, by contrast, expands outward. It demands action, retribution, resolution. It pushes you toward confrontation, sometimes recklessly, sometimes destructively. It tells you that the only way to restore balance is to lash out, to destroy what has hurt you, to assert control at any cost. Anger feels like strength, but it often leaves destruction in its wake—broken relationships, missed opportunities, deepened dissonance.

These emotions are not the enemy. Fear and anger exist for a reason. They are signals, designed to alert you to danger, to injustice, to imbalance. But when they take control, when they become the sole drivers of your choices, they lead you into patterns of reaction that don't align with your values or your goals. They perpetuate the very dissonance they are trying to protect you from.

The grip of fear and anger thrives in the absence of reflection. When emotions take over, there's no space to pause, to question, to choose. Every action becomes a reaction, every choice a reflex. And the more you react, the more dissonance you create, until the emotions that were meant to guide you leave you stuck in a cycle of chaos and confusion.

But emotions, as powerful as they feel, are not permanent. They are not unmovable. The grip of fear and anger begins to loosen when you create space—space to notice, to reflect, to ask yourself: *What am I feeling? Why am I feeling this? What do I truly need right now?* The act of noticing is the first step in reclaiming your agency, in shifting from reaction to intentional action.

Shifting the Grip

The grip of reactive emotions—fear, anger, resentment—feels absolute in the moment. They surge through you, consuming your thoughts, narrowing your focus, and demanding immediate action. Reactivity feels urgent, almost instinctive, like a force beyond your control. But reactive emotions, as powerful as they are, don't hold you as tightly as they seem to. Their power lies not in their presence but in your relationship to them.

Reactivity thrives on immediacy. It convinces you that you must act now, that pausing is dangerous, that reflection is weakness. It feeds on the belief that the only way to resolve dissonance is to respond immediately, forcefully, decisively. But this urgency is an illusion. The truth is, most moments of dissonance don't require immediate action—they require space. And in that space, the grip begins to loosen.

Shifting the grip of reactive emotions isn't about suppressing them or pretending they don't exist. It's about acknowledging them, naming them, and choosing how to respond to them. Fear is not your enemy—it's a signal. Anger is not a flaw— it's a messenger. Resentment is not weakness—it's a sign that something needs attention. These emotions don't need to be erased—they need to be understood.

The first step in shifting the grip is to pause. In the space of a pause, you create room to notice what's happening within you. You ask yourself: *What am I feeling? What triggered this? What is this emotion trying to tell me?* Fear might be pointing to a boundary that feels threatened. Anger might be highlighting a value that has been violated. Resentment might be revealing an unmet need. When you pause to listen, emotions shift from being overwhelming forces to being guides.

But pausing isn't always easy. Reactivity tells you that waiting is dangerous, that stillness is a risk. It takes courage to resist the pull of immediate action, to create a moment of stillness in the storm of emotion. Yet in that stillness, you find clarity. You move from reacting to choosing, from reflex to intention. You reclaim your agency, not by silencing your emotions, but by working with them.

The grip of reactive emotions loosens further when you connect with your values. Ask yourself: *What matters most to me in this moment? How can I act in alignment with what I truly want, rather than what my emotions are demanding?* This alignment doesn't mean ignoring your emotions—it means letting them inform your choices without dictating them. It means using fear, anger, and resentment as signals, not as masters.

To shift the grip of reactivity is not to eliminate emotion—it is to build a relationship with it. It is to see your emotions not as forces to be controlled, but as messages to be understood. The grip is strongest when you act without pausing, without reflecting, without connecting to what truly matters. But the moment you pause, the moment you listen, the moment you choose—you begin to reclaim yourself from the tyranny of reaction.

Section B: Reaction as Destruction
When Emotions Take the Wheel

When you act purely out of reaction, emotions become your drivers. They take the wheel and steer your actions, often without your consent or awareness. Fear pulls sharply to the left, avoiding risks at all costs. Anger slams on the gas, pushing you into confrontation before you've had time to think. Resentment turns the wheel again and again, keeping you circling the same frustrations without ever moving forward. These moments of reactivity feel powerful in the moment, but they often lead to outcomes that deepen dissonance rather than resolving it.

Reaction isn't action—it's reflex. It bypasses reflection, skipping over your values, your goals, your understanding of what truly matters. In its urgency, reaction sacrifices clarity for immediacy. It feels like doing something, but often it's just another way of staying stuck. A reactive word spoken in anger can damage a relationship. A decision made in fear can close off opportunities. A moment of frustration can leave ripples that stretch far beyond the moment itself.

The destructive power of reaction lies not in the emotions themselves but in the absence of pause. Fear isn't inherently harmful—it's a signal that something needs attention. Anger isn't destructive on its own—it's a response to a boundary being crossed or a value being violated. Resentment isn't inherently corrosive—it points to unmet needs or unresolved tensions. But when these emotions drive your actions without reflection, they amplify dissonance rather than addressing it.

This isn't about blaming yourself for being reactive—it's about understanding why reactivity happens and how it shapes the choices you make. Reactivity is a natural response to chaos, to overwhelm, to dissonance that feels unresolvable. It's your mind and body's way of trying to regain control, to create a sense of certainty in the midst of uncertainty. But control created through reaction is fragile. It often leaves behind more fractures than it mends.

To understand the destructive power of reaction is to understand the moments when emotions take the wheel. It's to look back at the times when your words or actions, driven by fear, anger, or resentment, created outcomes you didn't intend. It's not about judgment—it's about learning. What triggered the reaction? What were you trying to protect or achieve? And how might you respond differently if you had paused, even for a moment?

Choosing Reflection Over Reflex

The problem with reaction isn't the emotion behind it—it's the lack of reflection that follows. Emotions themselves are neither destructive nor harmful; they are signals. They arise to tell you that something needs attention: fear points to perceived threats, anger to violated boundaries, resentment to unmet needs. But when these emotions bypass reflection and leap directly to action, they often leave behind destruction, disconnection, and deepened dissonance.

Reaction feels satisfying in the moment. A sharp word spoken in anger feels like reclaiming power. A quick retreat driven by fear feels like self-preservation. A quiet withdrawal fueled by resentment feels like self-protection. But the satisfaction is fleeting, and the consequences often linger. Words spoken in haste can fracture trust. Avoidance can deepen misunderstandings. Withdrawal can widen gaps that were already too wide. Reaction solves nothing—it simply transfers the tension outward, leaving it unresolved.

To choose reflection over reflex is to create space between the emotion and the action. It's to pause, even for a moment, and ask yourself: *What am I feeling? Why am I feeling this? What do I want this action to achieve?* The pause doesn't erase the emotion—it allows you to work with it, to use it as information rather than letting it use you. Reflection isn't about suppressing emotion—it's about aligning your response with your values, your goals, your deeper understanding of what matters.

This space is where agency lives. It's where you reclaim the ability to choose how you respond, rather than being driven by reflex. It's where you remember that anger can be a signal without becoming a weapon, that fear can be a guide without becoming a cage, that resentment can point to unmet needs without becoming a wall between you and the people you care about. In the space of reflection, emotions become allies rather than tyrants.

Choosing reflection over reflex isn't always easy. The pull of reactivity is strong, especially in moments of heightened dissonance or chaos. But the act of pausing—even for a breath, even for a heartbeat—is an act of defiance against the tyranny of reaction. It's a reminder that you are not your emotions, that they do not control you, that you have the power to choose how you move forward.

The destruction of reaction isn't inevitable. It can be interrupted, redirected, transformed. It begins with noticing the moment when reflex wants to take over and choosing, instead, to pause. The pause is small, but its impact is profound. In that moment, you reclaim the ability to act, not from reflex, but from intention. And in doing so, you begin to create not just resolution, but alignment.

Chapter 9: The Mirror of Dissonance
Section A: Internal Chaos

The World Within

The chaos you see in the world isn't just out there—it's in here, within you. The tension you feel, the frustration, the overwhelm —they're not separate from the dissonance you perceive in the systems, relationships, and circumstances around you. They're reflections, each amplifying the other, creating a mirror effect where internal and external chaos feed into one another, making it harder to distinguish where one ends and the other begins.

Internal chaos is deeply personal, but it often mirrors broader patterns. The frustration you feel when you're stuck in an argument echoes the systemic conflicts you see in society. The overwhelm you feel at your responsibilities reflects the larger culture of endless demands and diminishing support. The disconnection you feel in your relationships parallels the isolation and fragmentation you see in the world. The mirror doesn't lie, but it does distort, magnifying both the chaos within and the chaos without.

This mirroring can be exhausting. It creates a loop where your internal struggles feel amplified by the external world, and the external chaos feels amplified by your internal state. You may feel stuck in this loop, unable to quiet the noise around you or the noise within you. But the mirror is not a trap—it's an opportunity. It's a chance to see the connections, to notice the patterns, to ask: *What is the chaos within me trying to show me about the world I inhabit? What is the chaos in the world reflecting back about what I need to address within myself?*

To confront internal chaos is not to fight it, but to understand it. It's to ask: *What am I holding onto that's adding to this tension? What patterns in my thinking, my behavior, my relationships are contributing to the dissonance I feel? What stories am I telling myself about what's possible, what's acceptable, what's inevitable?* Internal chaos doesn't arise from nowhere. It has roots—roots that can be traced, untangled, and gently re-aligned.

The mirror of dissonance doesn't just reflect what's wrong—it reflects what needs attention. The overwhelm you feel may point to the need for boundaries, for rest, for clarity about what truly matters. The frustration may point to values you hold dear, boundaries that have been crossed, or fears that need to be addressed. The disconnection may point to a longing for connection, a desire for authenticity, a hunger for something real. Chaos doesn't just reflect your struggles—it reflects your needs.

The Path to Understanding

When you begin to look into the mirror of dissonance, the first thing you see is the chaos. It's loud, overwhelming, and insistent, demanding your attention but offering no clear answers. The temptation is to turn away, to let the reflection blur, to focus on anything else. But the mirror doesn't go away, and the chaos doesn't quiet itself. To understand the reflection, you have to stay with it. You have to look closer.

The chaos within isn't random. It feels overwhelming because it's unresolved, because it's a collection of unspoken truths, unmet needs, and unexplored fears. It's the part of you that has been waiting for your attention, growing louder the longer it's been ignored. To understand it is to ask, *What is this chaos trying to tell me? What patterns in my life are contributing to it? What would it mean to listen instead of resist?*

Listening to your internal chaos is uncomfortable. It asks you to sit with the things you'd rather avoid—the fear of failure, the pain of disconnection, the uncertainty about who you are or where you're going. But discomfort is not the enemy. It's the starting point. Discomfort is what tells you that something needs to shift, that there's a tension that needs resolving, a truth that needs hearing.

The path to understanding internal chaos isn't about finding immediate clarity. It's about creating space for exploration, for curiosity, for noticing the patterns that have been driving your thoughts and actions. It's about asking yourself: *What do I feel right now? What triggered this feeling? What am I afraid of? What am I longing for?* These questions don't offer instant answers, but they open the door to awareness. And awareness is where understanding begins.

Internal chaos often reflects the stories you tell yourself about who you are and what you're capable of. These stories might be old, inherited from your upbringing, your culture, your past experiences. *You have to be perfect to be loved. You can't trust anyone. You'll never be enough.* These stories create the dissonance you feel because they don't align with the deeper truth of who you are. To confront the chaos is to confront these stories, to question their validity, to ask what they've been protecting and what they've been holding you back from.

The path to understanding isn't linear. It loops, it doubles back, it meanders. But every step you take toward awareness is a step toward alignment. The mirror may reflect chaos, but it also reflects possibility—the possibility of seeing yourself more clearly, of understanding your needs more deeply, of moving toward a life that feels more whole. The chaos isn't here to punish you—it's here to teach you. And when you're ready to look closely, it has much to reveal.

Section B: Confronting the Shadow
Seeing What's Hidden

The shadow is the part of yourself you don't want to see. It's the part you hide, the part you suppress, the part you deny. It holds the fears you can't name, the desires you're ashamed of, the emotions you've been told are too much. But the shadow doesn't disappear just because you ignore it. It lingers, shaping your actions, your relationships, your sense of self in ways you don't always realize. The shadow is always there, waiting for you to notice it.

Confronting the shadow feels like standing in front of a door you've locked for years, a door you've convinced yourself leads to nothing worth exploring. But the shadow isn't something to fear. It's not your enemy—it's your teacher. It holds the parts of yourself you've left in the dark, the pieces you've disowned because they didn't fit the image of who you thought you should be. These pieces aren't flaws—they're truths. And to live fully, you have to be willing to see them.

The shadow shows up in subtle ways. It's the resentment that flares up when someone asks for your help because you've always been taught to say yes, even when it drains you. It's the anger you suppress because you've been told it's not appropriate, not productive, not safe. It's the envy you feel when someone else achieves something you've always wanted but were too afraid to pursue. These moments of discomfort are glimpses of the shadow, reflections of the parts of yourself that are asking to be heard.

To see the shadow is to acknowledge that you are not one thing—you are many. You are light and dark, courage and fear, hope and doubt. The parts of yourself you've hidden are no less real than the parts you show to the world. They are not weaknesses—they are pieces of the whole. And the more you push them away, the louder they become, influencing your choices and your relationships in ways you don't always understand.

Seeing the shadow isn't about judgment—it's about curiosity. It's about asking: *What am I avoiding? What parts of myself feel too painful or too vulnerable to face? What might these parts have to teach me if I were willing to look at them with compassion instead of fear?* The shadow doesn't need to be eradicated—it needs to be integrated. And that integration begins with the willingness to see what's been hidden.

Embracing What You Find

Once you've seen the shadow, the question becomes: *What now?* It's not enough to simply notice it—to recognize the fear, the anger, the unmet need lurking beneath the surface. To truly confront the shadow, you have to engage with it. You have to step closer, not to conquer it or make it disappear, but to understand it, to accept it, and to integrate it as part of the whole.

The shadow carries meaning. It is a messenger, a signal, pointing to the places within you that need attention. The anger you suppress may be showing you where a boundary has been crossed. The fear you avoid may be protecting a vulnerability you haven't yet acknowledged. The envy you feel may be reminding you of dreams you've abandoned. These signals aren't flaws—they're invitations to look deeper.

Engaging with the shadow isn't easy. It requires you to sit with discomfort, to hold the parts of yourself you've labeled as unacceptable or unworthy, and to ask: *Why are you here? What do you need me to know? What have you been protecting me from, and what have you been holding me back from?* These questions are acts of compassion, not judgment. They create space for the shadow to speak, to reveal the truths it carries.

The act of embracing the shadow doesn't mean agreeing with everything it shows you. It doesn't mean letting anger, fear, or envy take over. It means acknowledging that these emotions, these parts of yourself, have value. They are part of your humanity, part of your story. To reject them is to reject a piece of who you are. To embrace them is to say: *You are part of me, and I am learning how to live with all of myself.*

This integration transforms the shadow from something feared to something understood. It allows you to see yourself more clearly, not as a collection of fragmented parts, but as a dynamic whole. The shadow doesn't disappear, but it loses its power to control you from the dark. When you bring it into the light, it becomes part of your story, part of your strength, part of the depth that makes you who you are.

To embrace the shadow is to embrace complexity. It is to accept that you are not just one thing, but many. It is to see the cracks and the light, the fear and the courage, the flaws and the beauty, and to recognize that all of it belongs. The shadow doesn't make you less —it makes you more. It makes you whole.

Chapter 10: The Emergent Resolution
Section A: Harmony from Chaos

Listening to the Tension

Chaos doesn't resolve itself by being ignored. The fractures in your life, the dissonance that surrounds you, don't disappear because you wish them away. Instead, they linger, waiting for you to notice, to listen, to engage. Harmony doesn't emerge by erasing chaos—it emerges by working with it, by leaning into the tension and letting it teach you what needs to change.

Tension feels uncomfortable, but it's also instructive. It holds within it the story of what isn't aligned, of what isn't working, of what needs to shift. The discomfort you feel is a signal, pointing to the spaces in your life where growth is possible. To listen to the tension is to stop resisting it, to stop fighting against the discomfort and start asking: *What is this tension trying to tell me? What is it showing me about my values, my needs, my relationships?*

Listening to the tension means sitting with it long enough to see its patterns. What once felt like an overwhelming wave of chaos begins to reveal its contours, its shapes, its movements. The fractures aren't random—they're part of a system, part of a larger story about how you've been living and where you need to go. The tension doesn't arise to punish you—it arises to guide you.

This isn't an easy process. The instinct is to smooth over the tension as quickly as possible, to restore a sense of control, even if that control is temporary or superficial. But quick fixes don't lead to harmony—they lead to more dissonance. True harmony arises when you allow yourself to stay with the tension long enough to understand it, to work with it, to let it show you what needs to shift.

When you listen to the tension, you begin to see its patterns, its signals, its invitations. The discomfort becomes less about what's wrong and more about what's possible. The tension doesn't disappear, but it begins to transform. It becomes a bridge, connecting where you are to where you need to be. It becomes the foundation for harmony—not the absence of chaos, but the resolution of it into something meaningful.

Shaping the Patterns

Harmony doesn't arrive as a gift—it's something you create. It doesn't spring fully formed from chaos, nor does it come as a moment of sudden clarity where all the pieces fall into place. Harmony grows, slowly and deliberately, from the patterns you shape within the chaos. It emerges not from avoidance, but from engagement—not from eliminating tension, but from working with it until it reveals its deeper rhythm.

The patterns within chaos are not immediately obvious. At first, all you see are fragments—contradictions that seem irreconcilable, problems that feel unsolvable. But when you begin to shape those fragments, when you sit with the tension and notice its movements, its edges, its spaces, something begins to shift. The fractures stop feeling like failures and start feeling like openings, opportunities to create something new.

Shaping the patterns of chaos isn't about control—it's about collaboration. Chaos holds its own kind of wisdom, its own kind of rhythm. When you try to impose order on it, to force it into a shape that feels safe or familiar, you lose the opportunity to learn from it. But when you work with chaos, when you allow it to guide you while bringing your own intention and attention to the process, something remarkable happens. The tension begins to resolve, not because it disappears, but because it transforms.

This process requires patience. Harmony doesn't emerge on a timeline. It doesn't conform to your expectations or your sense of urgency. It asks you to stay present, to resist the temptation to rush toward solutions, and to trust that the work you're doing— the noticing, the listening, the shaping—is enough. It asks you to let go of perfection, to let the patterns reveal themselves slowly, naturally, as you engage with the chaos around you and within you.

Shaping harmony from chaos also requires curiosity. It asks you to approach the tension with a sense of wonder rather than judgment. Instead of asking, *Why is this happening?* or *What's wrong with me?* it invites you to ask, *What is this tension showing me? What possibilities are hidden within these fractures? What new connections might emerge if I allow the patterns to unfold?* These questions don't erase the discomfort, but they create space for something more—a sense of possibility, a sense of movement, a sense of growth.

The harmony that emerges from chaos is not a static state. It's not a place you arrive and stay forever. It's dynamic, alive, constantly shifting as you continue to grow and change. The patterns you shape today may not hold tomorrow, and that's not a failure— it's a feature of the process. Harmony is not the absence of chaos; it's the ability to work with chaos, to find the rhythm within the tension, to create something meaningful in the spaces where dissonance once thrived.

When you shape the patterns of chaos, you're not just resolving dissonance—you're creating depth. You're adding layers of meaning, connection, and understanding to your life. The fractures become part of the design, not flaws to be hidden but features that give the pattern its texture, its richness, its beauty. Chaos doesn't disappear—it becomes integrated. And in that integration, harmony begins to take shape.

Section B: Growth Through Conflict
The Catalyst of Tension

Conflict is uncomfortable. It creates tension, forces confrontation, and pulls us out of our comfort zones. At its worst, it feels like a breakdown, a rupture in relationships, in understanding, in stability. But conflict isn't just a disruption—it's a catalyst. It's a space where transformation becomes possible, where growth begins to take shape, not in spite of the tension, but because of it.

The discomfort of conflict holds within it a kind of urgency. It demands attention, asking you to engage with what's unresolved, unspoken, or unaligned. It doesn't allow you to stay still. It pushes, prods, provokes, forcing you to reckon with what's not working. This isn't easy work. It's messy and emotional and often painful. But within the discomfort lies a hidden potential: the opportunity to see something new, to understand something deeper, to create something better.

Conflict creates growth because it exposes the gaps—the spaces where alignment is missing, where boundaries have been crossed, where values have been compromised. It brings to the surface what might otherwise remain hidden, giving you the chance to address it. This process is not about winning or losing—it's about discovering what the tension has to teach you, about yourself, about others, about the world you inhabit.

But growth through conflict doesn't happen automatically. Conflict also has the potential to deepen dissonance, to create fractures that feel irreparable, to entrench misunderstandings and resentment. The difference lies in how you approach it. Conflict driven by reactivity, by the need to defend, attack, or control, often leaves destruction in its wake. But conflict approached with curiosity, reflection, and a willingness to listen can become a space for transformation.

The first step in engaging with conflict as a catalyst is to pause. Instead of reacting to the tension, step back and ask: *What is this conflict trying to show me? What values or needs are at stake? What might this tension be asking me to change or reconsider?* The act of pausing creates space for reflection, for understanding, for intentional action. It allows you to move from a place of reaction to a place of growth.

Conflict doesn't have to be a breaking point—it can be a turning point. It can be the moment when the tension becomes productive, when the fractures begin to reveal not just what's broken, but what's possible. It's not about avoiding the discomfort, but about leaning into it, about letting the tension guide you toward the growth it's asking for.

The Transformation Within

Conflict doesn't leave you unchanged. Whether it strengthens you or fractures you further depends on how you choose to engage with it. The tension that arises in conflict is not just a disruption —it's a signal. It points to boundaries that need to be reinforced, values that need to be clarified, or relationships that need to be redefined. Conflict isn't just something that happens to you—it's something that shapes you.

Growth through conflict requires courage. It's tempting to avoid the tension, to smooth over the disagreements, to settle for surface-level peace instead of engaging with the deeper dissonance. But avoidance doesn't resolve conflict—it prolongs it. The unresolved tension lingers beneath the surface, reemerging in other ways, in other moments, until it's finally addressed. To grow, you have to face the tension, to meet it with curiosity instead of fear, to ask: *What is this conflict here to teach me?*

Transformation doesn't come from winning a conflict or proving a point—it comes from listening. It comes from stepping into the discomfort with an open mind, willing to hear not just what the other person is saying, but what the conflict is saying about you. Growth through conflict isn't about being right—it's about being real. It's about being willing to hold the mirror up to yourself and ask, *What am I protecting? What am I afraid to let go of? What am I trying to preserve, and why does it matter?*

The transformation within doesn't mean the conflict disappears. It means the way you engage with it changes. Instead of reacting defensively, you begin to respond intentionally. Instead of seeing the other person as an opponent, you begin to see them as a collaborator in the process of understanding. Instead of viewing the tension as a threat, you begin to see it as an opportunity for growth.

Conflict teaches you about yourself, about the things you value, about the boundaries you need, about the changes you're ready to make. It reveals the parts of yourself that are still unaligned, still unresolved, still growing. The transformation within isn't about resolving the conflict perfectly—it's about using the conflict to evolve, to become more aware, more authentic, more aligned with who you want to be.

This growth doesn't happen instantly. It's a process, one that requires patience, reflection, and a willingness to make mistakes. But every moment of engagement, every choice to listen instead of react, every act of intentionality over reflex, brings you closer to clarity. The tension that once felt overwhelming becomes the foundation for something stronger—a relationship rebuilt, a boundary clarified, a value reaffirmed.

Conflict isn't the opposite of growth—it's the space where growth begins. It's not something to be feared or avoided—it's something to be met, to be worked with, to be transformed. And in that transformation, you don't just resolve the tension—you become stronger, deeper, more whole. The growth within doesn't erase the scars of conflict, but it turns them into markers of resilience, reminders of the courage it takes to confront tension and let it shape you into something new.

Chapter 11: NOT OK into OK
Section A: The Catalyst of Despair

Breaking Point or Turning Point

Despair feels like an end. It whispers that there's no way forward, no resolution, no possibility of change. It convinces you that the weight of what's broken is too heavy to carry, that the chaos is too great to navigate. But despair, as overwhelming as it feels, is not just a breaking point—it's also a turning point. It is the space where transformation becomes possible, not because despair disappears, but because it forces you to see what cannot continue.

Despair arises when the old ways of being no longer work. It emerges when the patterns you've relied on, the beliefs you've held, the strategies you've used to navigate the world fall apart. Despair isn't just the presence of pain—it's the absence of what once gave you a sense of control, stability, or direction. It is the moment when you realize that something fundamental has to change.

This realization is terrifying. It feels like freefall, like losing your grip on everything you thought you could hold onto. But it is also an opportunity. Despair clears the ground, creating space for something new to emerge. It forces you to confront the truths you've avoided, to see the fractures you've tried to ignore, to acknowledge the misalignments that have brought you here. And in that confrontation, transformation begins.

Despair is not the absence of hope—it is the space where hope is redefined. It asks you to let go of the old stories, the old expectations, the old ways of being that no longer serve you. It asks you to imagine something different, something better, something more aligned with who you are and who you are becoming. The turning point is not in avoiding despair, but in moving through it, in letting it guide you toward the changes it's asking for.

Finding Motion in the Stillness

Despair feels static. It roots you in place, filling every moment with a weight that presses down, making even the smallest movement feel impossible. It convinces you that the stillness is permanent, that the heaviness you feel is something you must carry forever. But despair isn't static—it's charged with potential energy. Beneath its weight lies the spark of motion, waiting for the moment when the stillness shifts.

The power of despair lies in its clarity. It strips away illusions, leaving you face to face with what isn't working, what cannot continue, what must change. It doesn't offer easy answers, but it removes distractions, forcing you to confront the raw truths of your experience. This confrontation is painful, but it's also essential. Despair isn't here to keep you in the dark—it's here to show you what needs your attention.

To find motion in despair is to sit with it long enough to understand its message. What is this heaviness trying to tell you? What patterns have led you here? What parts of yourself or your life have been asking for change, and what would it mean to honor those requests? Despair doesn't ask you to fix everything at once —it asks you to notice. To look closely at what feels broken, not with judgment, but with curiosity. To ask: *What does this moment of stillness make possible?*

The shift begins with the smallest movement. Despair tells you that nothing matters, that no action is worth the effort. But the act of moving—even in the smallest way—challenges that narrative. It reminds you that despair, as heavy as it feels, is not absolute. The first step might be as simple as reaching out to someone, naming the heaviness, or taking a single action that aligns with what you value. It's not about fixing everything—it's about remembering that motion is possible.

As you begin to move, the stillness begins to loosen its grip. The weight doesn't disappear, but it becomes lighter, more navigable.

Each small act of engagement creates momentum, building toward something larger. The clarity that despair forced you to face becomes the foundation for transformation. What once felt like an end begins to feel like a beginning—a place where something new can take root.

Despair isn't the enemy. It's a signal. It tells you where alignment is missing, where clarity is needed, where growth is possible. It doesn't hold you back—it shows you what's been holding you back. And when you begin to listen, when you begin to move, despair transforms. It becomes not a breaking point, but a turning point—a place where the path to *OK* begins.

Section B: Alchemy of Dissonance
Transforming the Tension

Dissonance is not meant to stay unresolved. It exists to spark change, to catalyze growth, to show you where alignment is missing and where it might be found. But resolving dissonance isn't about eliminating it. It's about transforming it, turning tension into clarity, conflict into understanding, chaos into harmony. This is the alchemy of dissonance: the process of turning what feels unbearable into something meaningful.

The first step in this transformation is to recognize dissonance for what it is: a signal, not a flaw. Dissonance isn't here to punish you or to break you—it's here to guide you. It arises when your values, actions, and circumstances are out of alignment, creating a tension that demands attention. That tension feels heavy, overwhelming, but it also carries within it the energy for change. The very discomfort you feel is the sign that something new is waiting to emerge.

Transformation begins when you stop resisting the tension and start working with it. Resisting dissonance—ignoring it, denying it, avoiding it—only deepens the divide, making the tension stronger and the chaos louder. But when you lean into the tension, when you allow yourself to feel it, to name it, to explore it, you begin to uncover its patterns, its purpose, its potential. The tension isn't random—it's a map, showing you where to focus your energy, where to bring your attention, where to begin the work of transformation.

The alchemy of dissonance doesn't happen all at once. It's a process, one that requires patience, curiosity, and a willingness to sit with what feels unresolved. It asks you to step back and ask: *What is this tension trying to teach me? What values are being challenged? What boundaries need to be redefined? What possibilities are hidden within this discomfort?* These questions don't resolve the tension immediately, but they create space for it to shift, for clarity to begin to emerge.

Transformation also requires action. Dissonance doesn't resolve itself through reflection alone—it requires movement, choice, engagement. This doesn't mean rushing toward solutions or forcing resolution where it hasn't naturally unfolded. It means taking intentional steps that align with what you've learned from the tension, steps that move you closer to clarity, even if they feel small or uncertain. Transformation isn't about perfection—it's about momentum.

The tension of dissonance, as uncomfortable as it feels, is a gift. It holds within it the energy for change, the clarity for growth, the foundation for something new. To transform dissonance is to engage with it fully, to listen to its signals, to let it guide you toward alignment. It's not about erasing the tension—it's about creating something meaningful from it.

Turning Lead into Gold

The transformation of dissonance into alignment is not unlike alchemy—the ancient art of turning base metals into gold. It's a process that requires patience, intention, and the willingness to engage with what feels unworkable, uncomfortable, or even impossible. The tension you feel, the dissonance that weighs on you, is the raw material. The work is in shaping it, refining it, allowing it to change you as you work to change it.

Dissonance, like raw ore, holds value that isn't immediately visible. On the surface, it feels jagged, heavy, unwieldy. It's easy to dismiss it as something to get rid of, to discard, to move on from. But dissonance, when worked with rather than avoided, reveals its hidden properties. It shows you where your values are strongest, where your boundaries need attention, where your growth is calling you forward. It is not the enemy—it is the material of transformation.

Turning dissonance into alignment begins with acknowledgment. You can't transform something you refuse to face. This doesn't mean embracing dissonance as permanent or defining—it means recognizing it as part of the process. What is this tension showing you? What fears, needs, or misalignments does it reflect? What patterns in your life have created or sustained it? To name dissonance is to give yourself a starting point, a way to begin working with it instead of being overwhelmed by it.

The second step is reflection. Transformation doesn't happen through force—it happens through understanding. This is where you ask the deeper questions: *What does this tension mean? What is it asking of me? What would alignment look like in this situation?* These questions create space for clarity, for the fragments of chaos to begin forming into something coherent, something meaningful. The reflection isn't about finding instant answers— it's about staying curious, staying open, staying engaged.

The final step is action. Alchemy isn't just about seeing the potential in the raw material—it's about doing the work to refine it, to shape it, to bring it into its fullest form. This doesn't mean resolving every tension perfectly or achieving perfect alignment overnight. It means taking small, intentional steps that move you closer to your values, your goals, your sense of self. It's about progress, not perfection.

Transformation through dissonance isn't linear. It loops, it doubles back, it surprises you with new tensions even as old ones begin to resolve. But each step you take, each choice you make in alignment with what you've learned, brings you closer to harmony. The dissonance doesn't disappear, but it becomes part of the whole—a note in the larger symphony, adding depth, richness, and texture to the harmony you're creating.

The alchemy of dissonance is the process of turning what feels heavy and unresolved into something meaningful, something aligned, something valuable. It's not about erasing the tension—it's about using it, shaping it, letting it shape you in return. It's about remembering that even in the midst of chaos, even when everything feels *Not OK*, there is the possibility of transformation. And with transformation, there is the possibility of *OK*.

Chapter 12: The Harmonic Whole
Section A: Embracing the Shadow

Seeing the Light in the Dark

Harmony doesn't emerge from ignoring what's difficult. It isn't built by erasing what feels painful or by denying the parts of yourself you've kept hidden. True harmony comes from integration—from weaving together all the pieces, even the ones you've avoided, even the ones you're afraid to see. The shadow isn't the opposite of harmony—it's an essential part of it.

The shadow holds the parts of yourself you've disowned: the fear you suppress, the anger you avoid, the desires you've been told are unacceptable. These parts don't disappear just because you push them into the dark. They linger, shaping your actions, your choices, your relationships, in ways you don't always recognize. The shadow doesn't leave you—it waits for you. And the longer you avoid it, the louder its influence becomes.

To embrace the shadow is to see it not as a threat, but as a part of the whole. It's to acknowledge that the parts of yourself you've hidden are still part of you, and they carry meaning. The fear might be protecting a vulnerability that needs care. The anger might be pointing to a boundary that needs attention. The desire might be revealing a need you haven't allowed yourself to explore. The shadow doesn't diminish you—it completes you. It adds depth, complexity, and richness to the story of who you are.

Seeing the shadow requires courage. It asks you to sit with the parts of yourself you've labelled as unworthy or unacceptable and to look at them with compassion instead of judgment. It asks you to ask: *What have I been avoiding? What truths about myself have I been unwilling to face? What would it mean to bring these parts of myself into the light?* These questions don't erase the discomfort, but they create space for understanding, for integration, for alignment.

The shadow isn't something to fix or overcome—it's something to understand. It's a teacher, a guide, a reflection of the parts of yourself that need your attention. To embrace the shadow is to see yourself fully, not just as the version of yourself you present to the world, but as the dynamic, layered, evolving being you truly are. The shadow doesn't make you less—it makes you whole.

Integrating the Darkness

To embrace the shadow is to move beyond the fear of it. The parts of yourself that you've hidden—the anger, the fear, the unmet needs—are not separate from you. They are part of the same whole, part of the same system of thoughts, emotions, and experiences that make you who you are. The shadow isn't an enemy to be defeated; it's a piece of you waiting to be understood, accepted, and integrated.

Integration begins with acknowledgment. You don't have to agree with everything the shadow shows you, but you do have to see it. What emotions have you pushed away because they felt too overwhelming to handle? What truths about yourself have you denied because they didn't fit the image you thought you had to maintain? These aren't flaws—they're signals, pointing to the spaces within you that need care and attention.

The act of integrating the shadow isn't about fixing yourself—it's about accepting yourself. It's about recognizing that the parts of you that feel the most uncomfortable are often the ones that hold the greatest potential for growth. The fear you've been avoiding might be protecting a vulnerability that's ready to be healed. The anger you've been suppressing might be pointing to a value that needs defending. The sadness you've been ignoring might be asking for space to be acknowledged and honored. The shadow holds these truths not to hurt you, but to help you.

Integration isn't instant. It's a process, one that unfolds over time as you learn to approach your shadow with curiosity instead of judgment. It means asking questions instead of making assumptions. *What is this feeling trying to tell me? What need is behind this reaction? What value or boundary is this emotion connected to?* These questions don't eliminate the shadow, but they give it a voice, a place in the larger conversation of who you are.

As the shadow becomes integrated, it stops feeling like a weight you have to carry and starts feeling like a resource you can draw from. The parts of yourself you once feared become sources of strength, resilience, and understanding. The anger that felt so uncontrollable becomes a tool for setting boundaries. The fear that held you back becomes a guide for identifying risks worth taking. The sadness that felt endless becomes a reminder of the depth of your capacity to care.

The shadow doesn't go away, but it changes. It becomes less about what's hidden and more about what's possible. It becomes part of the story, not as a flaw, but as a feature. The cracks in the mirror of your self-image don't disappear—they become the lines that give the reflection its depth, its texture, its truth. Integration doesn't mean perfection—it means wholeness.

To live with an integrated shadow is to live with a sense of harmony that holds both light and dark, both strength and vulnerability, both what you've known and what you're still discovering. The shadow doesn't define you, but it deepens you. It adds layers to the person you are, creating a fuller, richer, more authentic version of yourself. And in that authenticity, you find clarity, connection, and alignment.

Section B: Depth in Harmony
The Whole Greater Than Its Parts

Harmony isn't the absence of tension—it's the resolution of it. It's the process of bringing together all the fragments, the contradictions, the misalignments, and creating something larger, something fuller, something that holds all of it without breaking. True harmony doesn't erase the cracks—it deepens them, weaving them into the fabric of the whole, turning them into lines of connection rather than separation.

This depth doesn't come from avoiding what's uncomfortable. It comes from facing it, from integrating the dissonance rather than ignoring it. The fractures you've experienced, the tensions you've felt, the shadow you've come to know—these aren't obstacles to harmony; they are its foundation. They add complexity, texture, and richness to the life you're building. Without them, the harmony would be shallow, fragile, easily disrupted. With them, it becomes something resilient, something alive.

To embrace this depth is to see yourself not as a collection of separate pieces, but as a dynamic whole. The fear you've felt, the anger you've carried, the sadness you've endured—they're not weaknesses. They're threads in the larger tapestry of your experience, threads that weave together to create a pattern unique to you. Each emotion, each struggle, each moment of dissonance has a place in that pattern, a role in shaping the harmony of who you are.

The whole is greater than its parts because it holds the tension of those parts. It holds the contradictions, the imperfections, the unresolved questions, and it makes space for all of them to coexist. Harmony doesn't mean everything is resolved—it means everything is included. It means recognizing that the moments of chaos, the fractures in your relationships, the doubts in yourself are not separate from the clarity, the connection, the growth. They are all part of the same process, the same journey, the same whole.

This depth is what gives harmony its strength. It's what allows it to hold not just what's beautiful, but what's difficult. It's what allows it to adapt, to evolve, to grow as you grow. Harmony isn't a fixed state—it's a living one, constantly shifting to include the new tensions, the new questions, the new truths that arise as you move through life. Its depth isn't something you achieve once —it's something you cultivate, moment by moment, choice by choice, reflection by reflection.

The Beauty of Complexity

Harmony isn't about simplicity. It's about depth, richness, and the interplay of contrasts. True harmony doesn't erase the complexity of life—it embraces it. It acknowledges that the dissonance, the tension, the unresolved parts of your story are not failures. They are what give the whole its beauty, its meaning, its truth.

The cracks, the fractures, the shadows—they don't diminish harmony. They deepen it. They add texture, turning a flat image into a multidimensional reality. Without the tension of dissonance, harmony would be shallow, lifeless, without substance. But with it, harmony becomes something vibrant, something that resonates not because it's perfect, but because it holds everything—the light and the dark, the joy and the sorrow, the questions and the answers.

To find beauty in complexity is to let go of the idea that harmony is about fixing or finishing. Harmony isn't a destination—it's a process. It's the act of weaving together all the pieces, all the contradictions, all the moments of chaos, and creating something that holds them all without collapsing. It's about seeing the tension not as something to be resolved once and for all, but as something to be worked with, something to be integrated, something to be celebrated.

This process isn't easy. It asks you to see the parts of yourself and your life that you've avoided, to sit with the discomfort of dissonance, and to trust that the work of integration is worth it. It asks you to believe that the fractures don't define you, but they do shape you. And in that shaping, they create something unique, something beautiful, something whole.

Harmony doesn't mean the tension disappears—it means the tension finds its place. It becomes part of the greater whole, part of the rhythm and movement that makes life dynamic and alive. The beauty of harmony lies in its complexity, in its ability to hold the contradictions, the imperfections, the unresolved truths, and still create something that feels meaningful.

This is the depth of harmony: not a static state of perfection, but a living process of integration and growth. It's about creating a whole that is greater than the sum of its parts, a life that holds both the pain and the joy, both the struggle and the triumph, both the *Not OK* and the *OK*. It's about seeing that the beauty of your story isn't in its resolution, but in its unfolding, its evolution, its endless capacity to grow.

The harmonic whole isn't about erasing who you've been or what you've experienced. It's about including all of it, weaving it together into something that is uniquely yours. The fractures, the shadows, the tensions—they are not mistakes. They are the lines of connection, the places where light enters, the spaces where harmony begins. And when you embrace them, when you see them for what they are, you create a harmony that is as deep, as complex, and as beautiful as life itself.

B.T.C.

18-12-24

Epilogue:
The Song Within the Dissonance

Dissonance doesn't vanish. It doesn't dissolve into nothingness or resolve into a static state of perfection. It remains, woven into the fabric of your life, a reminder that harmony is not the absence of tension but the integration of it. The work you've done—the reflection, the patience, the small acts of alignment—is not about erasing dissonance. It's about learning to live with it, to work with it, to let it deepen the melody of who you are.

The chaos that once felt overwhelming now feels different. It's not that it's gone—it's that it no longer controls you. The fractures you once avoided have become openings, spaces where growth has taken root. The shadows you once feared have become guides, showing you the parts of yourself you needed to see. The tension you once resisted has become a rhythm, a movement that carries you forward.

This isn't the end of the journey—it's another beginning. The process of turning *Not OK* into *OK* is ongoing, a dynamic, ever-evolving dance between what feels unresolved and what is coming into alignment. The path isn't linear, and it isn't always clear. There will be moments when the dissonance feels heavy again, when the tension rises, when the void whispers its familiar call. But now you know something you didn't know before: the dissonance is not your enemy. It's part of the song.

To live with dissonance is to live with motion. It's to understand that harmony isn't static—it's something you create, moment by moment, choice by choice. It's to accept that the fractures, the shadows, the chaos will always be there, not as flaws, but as features of a life that is real, that is whole, that is alive. The cracks in the mirror of your life don't diminish its reflection—they make it more beautiful, more true.

As you move forward, the question isn't whether the tension will return—it's how you will respond to it. Will you resist it, or will you let it guide you? Will you see it as a sign of failure, or will you see it as a signal of growth? The work you've done here, the insights you've gained, have given you the tools to choose. The dissonance may remain, but so does your capacity to create harmony within it.

This is the song within the dissonance: the reminder that life is not about erasing tension, but about embracing it. It's about seeing the fractures not as endings, but as beginnings. It's about finding the rhythm within the chaos, the light within the shadow, the alignment within the tension. It's about remembering that *Not OK* is not the opposite of *OK*—it's part of it. It's part of the whole.

And in that whole, there is beauty. There is meaning. There is you. The song isn't finished, but it's playing. And as you listen, as you create, as you move through the dissonance, you are not just hearing the harmony—you are becoming it.

Aimee,
I hope you need
these words rarely.
Be kind to you!
— Brooke

Printed in Great Britain
by Amazon